WHAT
MAKES THE
POPCORN 'POP'?

Om
KIDZ

An imprint of Om Books International

Contents

- What makes cola fizzy? — 3
- What are soap bubbles made of? — 3
- What makes fireworks colourful? — 4
- What makes flames point upwards? — 4
- What is air made of? — 5
- What happens when I blow up a balloon and let it go? — 5
- What causes me to slip when I step on ice? — 6
- What makes glue stick things? — 6
- What makes my right hand look like it is the left one in the mirror? — 7
- What makes me see through glass door but not a wall? — 7
- What makes the popcorn pop? — 8
- What makes water droplets dance on a hot pan? — 8
- What keeps me from floating in air? — 9
- What makes a ship float on water? — 9
- What turns milk sour? — 10
- What makes apples turn brown when cut? — 10
- What changes water into ice? — 11
- What helps me pull out water with a straw? — 11
- What gives rainbow its seven colours? — 12
- What makes the sky look blue? — 12
- What makes an egg hard inside when it is boiled? — 13
- What makes a ball bounce? — 13
- What is an easy way to lift heavy objects? — 14
- What magic makes a key open a lock? — 14
- What is the secret of shadows? — 15
- What makes bits of paper stick to a plastic comb? — 15
- Index — 16

What makes cola fizzy?

It's the carbon dioxide! Cola has carbon dioxide gas dissolved in it. When the bottle is closed, the cola is under pressure, and so carbon dioxide does not escape the bottle. But when you open the bottle, it releases the pressure and carbon dioxide begins to escape in the form of rising bubbles. This is what makes cola fizzy. So, if you want your cola to fizz, keep the bottle shut!

Pocket fact

The first flavoured soft drink was made in the United States in 1807 by Townsend Speakman. The popular ingredients in the drink were birch bark, dandelions, ginger, lemon, coca, and kola!

Try this

- Collect two pipe cleaners and soap water.
- Bend a pipe cleaner into a square and wrap the ends to hold it together.
- Now fold the other pipe cleaner in half and loop it around one side of the square.
- Twist the ends together to make a handle and use it as a bubble blower.
- Dip the bubble blower into the soap water and slowly blow through it.

What are soap bubbles made of?

Air wrapped in a soap film! A bubble is a pocket of soap and water filled with air. When soap and water mix together and air blows into it, a thin skin traps the air. This is what makes a bubble. A bubble has soap molecules all over its surface. A thin layer of water lies between the two layers of soap molecules. They work together to hold the air inside the bubble and make them float.

What makes fireworks colourful?

Chemicals! All fireworks are made of different chemicals. These chemicals glow in different colours when they are hot. Fireworks that contain the chemical sodium glow with a yellow and orange colour. Those with potassium give out a purple glow, and those with iron, magnesium and aluminium glow in white and golden colours.

Find out

Why do fireworks make sound when they burn?

Pocket fact

Have you ever wondered what a flame would look like without gravity? Will it point upwards? The answer is no! The flame would appear round and blue in absence of gravity.

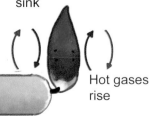

Cooler gases sink

Hot gases rise

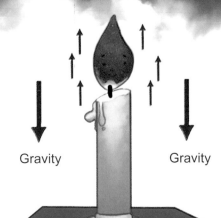

Gravity   Gravity

What makes flames point upwards?

Its low density! Flames are hot gases that emit light. As a flame burns, it heats the surrounding gases. The hot air around the flame pushes up as it is less dense. Cool air is pulled down by gravity and gets closer to the flame and replaces the lighter gases that are pushed up. This makes the flame point upwards.

Air is made up of different gases. Nitrogen accounts for 78% of the air, 21% of it is oxygen, essential for our survival. So what makes up the other 1%? Besides oxygen and nitrogen, air also has small amounts of other gases, like carbon dioxide, neon, helium, methane etc. You'll also find water vapour, pollen, dust, and even microbes in it!

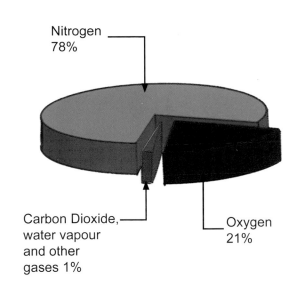

Nitrogen 78%

Carbon Dioxide, water vapour and other gases 1%

Oxygen 21%

Reaction: Balloon goes up

Action: Air rushes down

Find out

Air has oxygen that is essential for breathing. What is the use of nitrogen?

What happens when I blow up a balloon and let it go?

When you blow a balloon, air occupies the space inside it and the balloon expands in size. The air then pushes against the inner surface of the balloon, building a pressure. The outside pressure balances the pressure inside. But when you let it go, the balloon quickly releases air and moves in the opposite direction.

Pocket fact

Swedish pharmacist Carl Wilhelm Scheele, British clergyman Joseph Priestley and French chemist Antoine Laurent Lavoisier, researched and discovered oxygen between 1770 and 1780. The name 'oxygen' was first used by Lavoisier in 1777.

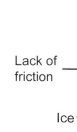

What causes me to slip when I step on ice?

Lack of friction

Ice

The lack of friction! Friction is a force that occurs when two rough surfaces rub together. When the surfaces come in contact, they press up against each other and cause friction that helps you walk. But sometimes, a surface like ice may be smooth and lacks the roughness that you need to stay upright, this makes it very slippery to walk on.

Find out

We get natural adhesive from some trees. Can you name two such trees?

Pocket fact

Get, set, go!
When vehicles move, the air around them generates friction called air resistance that slows them down. Fast moving vehicles, such as cars, trains, and airplanes are all designed with curved and sloping surfaces so that they can reduce the drag. This helps them to move faster and consume less fuel.

What makes glue stick things?

Glue is made from a fluid that changes to a solid state when it is dry. Most of the things that can be glued together have tiny ridges and bumps on their surface. When you apply glue to such a surface, it fills in all the ridges and bumps. Once the glue dries, it works like a strong bond grabbing hold of the two surfaces to keep it together.

Mirror

You looking into mirror

What makes my right hand look like it is the left one in the mirror?

A mirror reflects exactly what is in front of it. When you stand in front of a mirror, light rays reflected by your left hand fall on the mirror and make a reflection straight at the spot where it falls. Similarly, rays from your right hand also follow the same reflection method. So, your right becomes left and left becomes right in the mirror. It is just the same as your friend standing opposite you holding your hands.

Try this

What would these letters look like when you see them in a mirror? The first one has been done for you.

F Ⅎ   J
B   A

What makes me see through glass door but not a wall?

Light! Light travels in a straight line and is reflected and absorbed by different objects. Since a glass door is transparent, light easily passes through it and we can see what is on the other side. When light falls on a wall, it is absorbed by the wall and cannot pass through it. So, we are unable to see what is on the other side of the wall.

A tiny drop of water! Popcorn is not ordinary corn. It is the only type of corn that pops. Each grain of popcorn has a tiny droplet of water inside it, surrounded by a hard cover called hull. As you heat the popcorn, the water turns into steam. Since the steam can't escape the hard cover, the grain of corn pops.

Find out
What do you call water when it changes from liquid to gas?

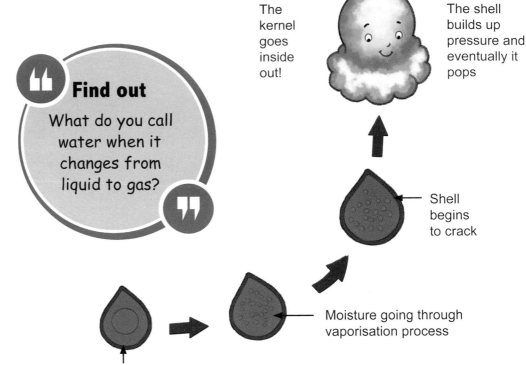

The kernel goes inside out!

The shell builds up pressure and eventually it pops

Shell begins to crack

Moisture going through vaporisation process

Each kernel holds 13% moisture in order to pop.

Pocket fact
Popcorn becomes mobile!
An inventor named Charles Cretors introduced the first moveable popcorn machine in 1893. The machine was introduced at the World's Columbian Exposition in Chicago.

POP CORN

What makes water droplets dance on a hot pan?

The droplets dance because they vaporise immediately on contact with the hot plate! When you sprinkle water on a hot pan, it forms an invisible layer that prevents it from boiling quickly. Due to this, drops of water hover over the surface of the pan. This makes the drops skid around the pan and it seems to dance!

What keeps me from floating in air?

Gravity pulls you down! Gravity is an invisible force that attracts any two objects found in the universe. The heavier the object, the stronger is its gravitational pull. Our planet, Earth, is very heavy and so it has a very strong gravitational pull. This makes everything on Earth stay in place and keeps you from floating in air.

Gravity

Gravity

Pocket fact

Lowest gravity on Earth! Parts of Hudson Bay and the surrounding regions of Quebec are areas with very low gravity on Earth.

Try this

Collect any 10 items, five of which you think will float on water and five that will sink. Take a bucket full of water and drop each of the 10 items one-by-one. Was your guess correct?

What makes a ship float on water?

Water's high density! Ships can float because they are less dense than water. When a ship is on water, two forces act upon it: a downward force of the ship and an upward force that's determined by the weight of the water displaced by the ship. When this upward force is more than the weight of the ship, it makes the ship float!

Ship's mass: 1000kg

Air in ship

Displaced water

What turns milk sour?

An acid! Milk contains a type of sugar called lactose. When milk is boiled and stored in a cool place, lactobacillus, the bacteria present in milk, are killed and milk does not turn sour. But when milk is not boiled or left in a humid place, the bacteria grows easily, causing lactose to react with oxygen. This makes lactic acid. It is this lactic acid that turns milk sour.

Find out
Why do fruits rot?

Lacto Bacillus makes Lactic Acid

Pocket fact

Helpful bacteria!
Lactobacillus bacteria are not always harmful. This bacteria at the right temperature can change milk to curd!

What makes apples turn brown when cut?

A reaction with air! Apples and some other fruits contain an enzyme called tyrosinase. When apples are cut, this enzyme reacts with oxygen in the air and the iron-rich chemicals present in the apple. This reaction forms a brown coating on the surface of the apples.

What changes water into ice?

Loss of heat at 0° Celsius! Water is made of tiny particles called molecules. When water gets colder than 0° Celsius, the molecules of water lose their energy. This brings them closer together and makes them move slow. They then form a hexagonal pattern turning water into ice.

Pocket fact

Have you heard of anything that can change air into water? There's a billboard in Peru that creates drinkable water out of thin air!

Find out

What is water made of?

What helps me pull out water with a straw?

It's the air pressure! When you drink water using a straw, you create a vacuum by sucking the air out of it. Since there is air outside, it creates pressure around the straw. The outside pressure of the straw is greater than the pressure inside. This pressure causes water to rise up in the straw and gets pulled into your mouth.

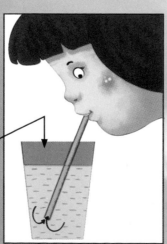

Atmospheric Pressure

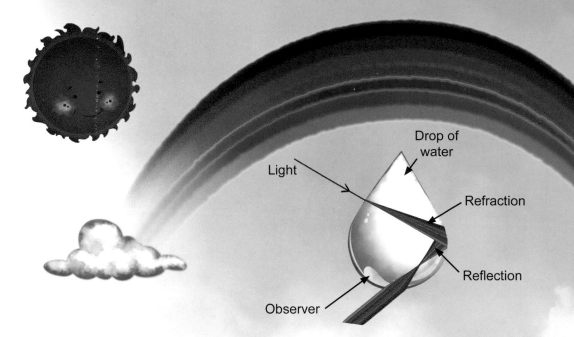

Drop of water

Light

Refraction

Reflection

Observer

What gives rainbow its seven colours?

Splitting of the sunlight! Sunlight is made of different colours but we cannot see them easily. When we pass sunlight through a prism or glass, it splits into a band of seven colours called spectrum. When it rains, raindrops act as tiny prisms. When sunlight passes through them, it breaks up into its spectrum and we see all the colours in the form of a rainbow.

Find out

Why does the sky appear black at night even when there is moon to give light?

Pocket fact

Moonbows!
Moonbows are like rainbows which occur when the moon's light reflects through raindrops. This type of rainbow is rare because the moon's light usually isn't bright enough for a rainbow to form.

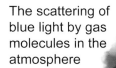

The scattering of blue light by gas molecules in the atmosphere

Sunlight made of all colours

What makes the sky look blue?

It's the Sun! Blue colour in the sunlight spectrum travels in the form of short and small waves. When sunlight reaches the Earth's atmosphere, it gets scattered in all directions by the gases and particles in the Earth's air. This is what gives sky its blue colour in the day.

What makes an egg hard inside when it is boiled?

Eggs are made of proteins. When you boil an egg, the protein molecules get heated up and gain energy. It then forms strong bonds with all the other protein molecules around it. This is what we see as a hard, boiled egg!

Find out

What is an egg shell made of?

Pocket fact

Ping pong balls bounce higher than other balls. Table tennis players started using ping pong balls made of cellulose after James Gibb discovered the celluloid ball during a trip to the United States in 1901.

What makes a ball bounce?

Gravity and energy! Gravity pulls everything down towards the Earth. But when the ball falls down, it picks up energy before it reaches the ground and this energy needs to be used. So, when the ball touches the ground, the energy inside the ball pushes it and the ball bounces.

What is an easy way to lift heavy objects?

Pulleys! Sometimes it's not easy to lift heavy objects. This problem can be fixed with the help of a simple machine, like a pulley. A pulley consists of a wheel on a fixed axle, with a groove along the edges to guide a rope. It helps you lift heavy objects easily. When you put two or more wheels together, and run a rope around them, a great lifting machine is created!

Pulley

Effect

Rope

Load

W

Find out

Are there any locks that can be opened without a key?

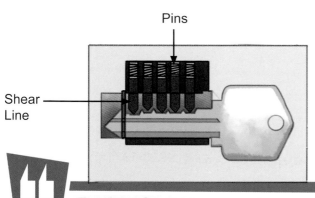

Pins

Shear Line

Pocket fact

We all take the credit!
Many people are credited with inventions of different locks. Just have a look.
Robert Barron in 1778 : double-acting tumbler lock
Joseph Bramah in 1784 : Bramah lock, unpickable for 67 years
Jeremiah Chubb in 1818 : detector lock with high internal security
Linus Yale, Sr. in 1848: first pin tumbler lock
James Sargent in 1857 and 1873 : first combination lock and first time lock mechanism
Samuel Segal in 1916 : first jemmy-proof lock
Harry Soref in 1924 : first padlock

What magic makes a key open a lock?

It's the teeth on the keys! Every key has a unique pattern of cuts or teeth that make it open the lock it belongs to. A lock has a track called shear line inside it. This shear line has spring-loaded pins that move up and down. The pattern on every key matches up to the pins on the inside of its lock. When the teeth fit into the shear line, the lock opens! When the teeth don't match up with the pins, the lock doesn't turn and a different key is needed!

What is the secret of shadows?

It's light blocked by objects! Light travels in a straight line and cannot pass through opaque objects. Since light cannot pass through the object, it creates a dark patch around it. This area where the light cannot reach is called a shadow.

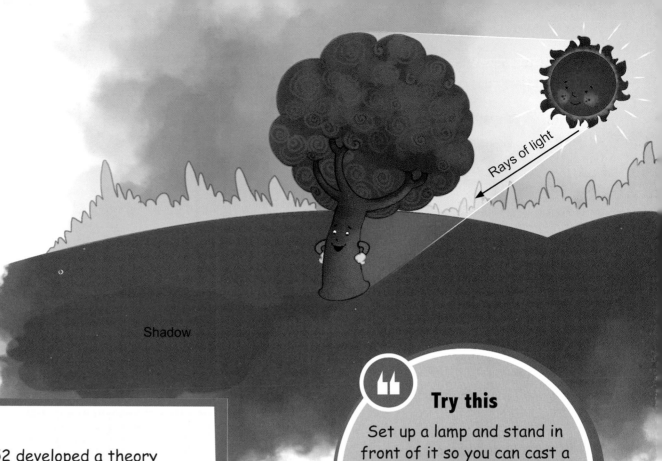

Rays of light

Shadow

Pocket fact

Ben Franklin in 1752 developed a theory that lightning in the sky was the same static electricity that is generated by rubbing a comb on dry hair. He performed a kite experiment to test this which later came to be known as Franklin's famous kite experiment.

Try this

Set up a lamp and stand in front of it so you can cast a shadow on the wall behind you. Watch your shadow carefully. What happens when you move closer to the lamp or move away from it?

What makes bits of paper stick to a plastic comb?

Static electricity! When you run a plastic comb through your dry hair several times and bring it near bits of paper, they stick to the comb. When you run the comb on your hair, it gets charged and acquires a force in the form of static electricity. This pulls the bits of paper towards the comb.

Index

A, B

absorbed 7
acquires 15
aluminum 4
attractive 15
axle 14
bacteria 10
balloon 5
bounce 13
bubble 3
bumps 6

C, D

carbon dioxide 3
charged 15
chemicals 4
coating 10
colours 4
cover 8
dark 15
density 4
displaced 9
dissolved 3
droplet 8
dust 5

E, F

energy 11
enzyme 10
escape 3
fireworks 4
fizz 3
flame 4
float 3
fluid 6
friction 6

G, H, I

glue 6
grain 8
gravity 4
groove 14
helium 5
hexagonal 11
hull 8
humid 10
invisible 8
iron 4

L, M

Lactic acid 10
lactobacillus 10
lactose 10
layer 3
magnesium 4
methane 5
microbes 5
mirror 7
molecules 3

N, O, P

neon 5
opaque 15
oxygen 5
particles 11
patch 15
pattern 11
pollen 5
popcorn 8
potassium 4
pressure 3
prism 12
proteins 13
pulleys 14

R, S, T

rainbow 12
reflects 7
ridges 6
rough 6
roughness 6
scattered 12
shadow 15
shear 14
skid 8
sodium 4
sour 10
spectrum 12
static electricity 15
straw 11
surfaces 6
transparent 7
traps 3
tyrosinase 10

U, V, W

unique 14
universe 9
upward 9
vacuum 11
water vapour 5
waves 12
wheels 14